PLAY and LEARN

year old

56 simple activities

Learn while having fun

Quality time for parents and children

The activities in this book are organized into the following sections:

Special thanks to Joan Henry and Jean Tuemmler, my Mulberry Tree teaching team.

Congratulations on your purchase of some of the finest teaching materials in the world.

For information about other Evan-Moor products, call 1-800-777-4362 or FAX 1-800-777-4332

Visit our website http://www.evan-moor.com. Check the Product Updates link for supplements, additions, and corrections for this book.

Author: Jill Norris
Editor: Marilyn Evans
Copy Editor: Cathy Harber
Illustrator: Cindy Davis
Designer: Cheryl Puckett
Desktop: Carolina Caird
Cover: Cheryl Puckett

Evan-Moor
EDUCATIONAL PUBLISHERS

EMC 4500

How to Play and Learn with Your One-Year-Old

What can I do to help my one-year-old learn and have fun at the same time? This book answers that question with 56 simple activities that parents can do as they spend quality time with their one-year-olds. Each activity is fun *and* provides a positive learning experience.

Play and learn at bath time or when you're waiting in line. Have activities ready if you're riding in the car and when your child is getting ready for bed. Sitting at the table, playing outside, or sharing a story—wherever you are and whatever you're doing—you can provide the kinds of experiences that build the foundation for future learning.

Use this book as a resource. Read over the activities to become familiar with them, but don't worry about doing them precisely. Enjoy the special time you spend with your child and remember:

- **One-year-olds may love to be independent.**
  Control your child's activities by controlling the environment.

- **One-year-olds can be tireless explorers.**
  Support your child's explorations, both physical and mental, by exploring alongside.

- **One-year-olds may enjoy motion.**
  Strollers, backpacks, and wagons will make your travels more fun.

- **One-year-olds can entertain an audience.**
  Children appreciate applause as they demonstrate their latest accomplishments.
  (show waving bye-bye or playing pat-a-cake)

The intellectual and social stimulation that you provide as your child grows is important. Spend time with your one-year-old.

- Talk to your child.
- Play with your child.
- Read to your child.

Helping your child learn about the world is easy and fun!

A Note about Reading
The most important thing you can do for your child is **read**. The time from twelve to eighteen months is not too soon to start. Some children will be ready to listen sooner than others, but at least try reading to your child. If he or she shows little interest, try again in another week or two or try parallel reading (page 76). Remember that any time of day is a good time to read.

Building Blocks to Learning

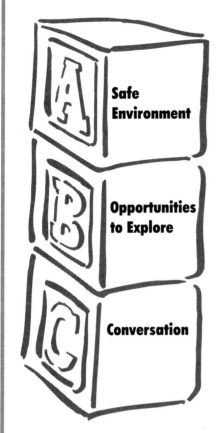

Safe Environment

Opportunities to Explore

Conversation

One-year-olds do not think ahead about what they are going to do. Instead, they move around a room almost at random, stopping to investigate briefly whatever they come in contact with. Your job is to provide stimulating toys and objects, to find out what your child likes to do best, and to do it often.

One-year-olds lug, tug, dump, push, pound, and move things. They will endlessly shift their attention from a pull-toy to a chair to a stuffed rabbit to pots and pans to balls to blocks to a wagon. They fill pails with sand and then dump the sand out. Provide as many opportunities as possible for your child that emphasize physical activity.

Encourage one-year-olds to show you things and then talk with them about what they show you. Take them on a stroller ride and point out interesting things along the way — dogs, babies, airplanes, and mud puddles. Carry on conversations not for teaching, but simply as part of your routine.

Skills for Success

Each page in *Play and Learn* is labeled to tell which skill areas are developed by the activity. Often a single activity addresses several different skills. You help to build the foundation for your child's success in school when you provide practice in these six important skills:

 Large-Motor Development
walking, running, jumping, large-muscle movement

 Coordination and Dexterity
small-muscle movements in the hands and fingers

 Language Development
speaking, listening, and developing vocabulary

 Creativity
imagining, exploring different materials, thinking in new ways

 Problem Solving
finding alternative solutions, understanding cause and effect

 Memory and Concentration
remembering, connecting different ideas

Bath Time

Rub-a-dub-dub.
Have fun in the tub.

Splashing about
I learn as you scrub.

Play and Learn to

- explore cause and effect
- develop vocabulary
- develop visual ability
- sharpen conceptual thinking
- practice fine-motor coordination

Activities

Wash Your Face

Use a washcloth to wipe your face.

What You Need

- bathtub and water
- washcloth

What You Do

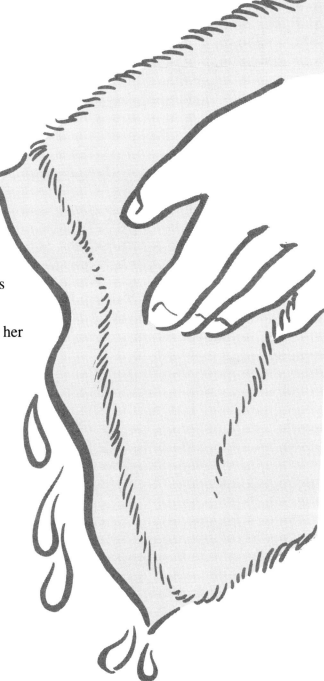

1. Give your child a small washcloth to hold as you use another for washing.

2. Wipe child's face and say, *Wash your face*.

3. Applaud when child imitates you and washes his or her face.

Encourage your child to wash other parts of his or her body by modeling the washing.

> Be ready for a role-reversal. My daughter Amy parroted, "Wash your face!" and smeared her washcloth across my face. We dripped and laughed together.

The Parts of My Body

Name the parts of the body as you wash.

What You Need

- one wet child

What You Do

1. Wash a toe. Say,
   This is a toe.

2. Repeat using different body parts.

3. As your child is ready, follow with
   Show me a toe.

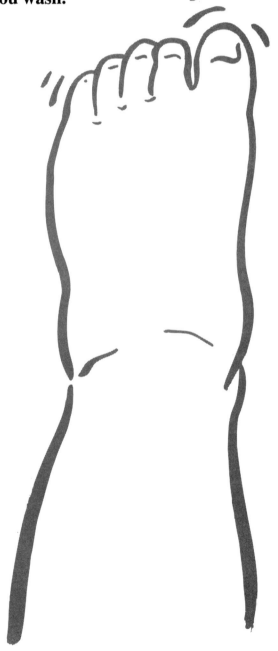

Sponge Play

Lifting, splashing, dripping, squeezing—a sponge is fun.

What You Need

- two small sponges or foam balls
- tub of water

What You Do

1. Give a sponge to your child. Keep one for yourself.

2. Show how you:
   dip the sponge into the water
   lift it high
   splash it down
   squeeze it

3. Let your child try out sponge play.

*Note: Applaud and name the things your child chooses to do.
Don't insist that the things you did be repeated.*

> Think of new ways to
> have fun with a sponge.

     Play and Learn with Your One-Year-Old • EMC 4500

Pick It Up, Please

Your child retrieves objects from the bottom of the tub.

What You Need

- easy-to-grasp, waterproof objects
    - rubber car
    - squeeze animal
    - jar ring
    - rattle

- tub of water

What You Do

1. Drop object(s) in the water. Ask your child to pick it up.

2. Applaud success.

Scoop and Pour

Provide a cup for scooping and pouring.

What You Need

• small plastic cup with a handle

What You Do

1. Scoop and pour with the cup several times.

2. Put the cup in the tub so that your child can scoop and pour.

3. Add words to the actions.

If your child doesn't choose to scoop, don't force the issue. Keep the cup close by and try again another time.

Count Those Toes

Count clean toes and other body parts.

What You Need

- a clean child
- a big towel

What You Do

1. Make a game out of counting body parts as you dry off your child.
   Look, here are some clean toes.
   How many are there?
   1–2–3–4–5–6–7–8–9–10
   10 clean toes.

2. Repeat with other body parts.
   Here's a clean ear.
   How many ears?
   1–2
   2 clean ears.

Take It Off

Undressing is great fun.

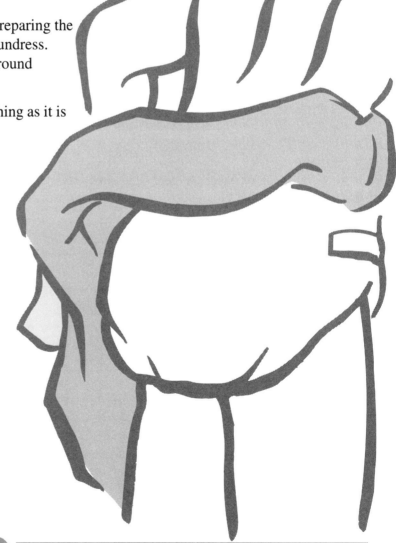

What You Need

• a fully clothed toddler

What You Do

1. Allow enough time while you are preparing the water in the tub to have your child undress. One-year-olds (particularly those around 15 months) love independence.

2. Say the name of each article of clothing as it is taken off.
   There goes a shoe.
   There goes a sock.

If your child isn't ready to undress independently, help with the task.

Pin, Please

Give your child a job during the getting-dressed process.

What You Need

- safety diaper pin
- pair of socks or similar item

What You Do

1. As you dress your child, have him or her hold one item that will be needed.

2. When it's time to use the item, say, *(name of item), please.*

3. Your child then hands it over to you.

Try this with more than one item.

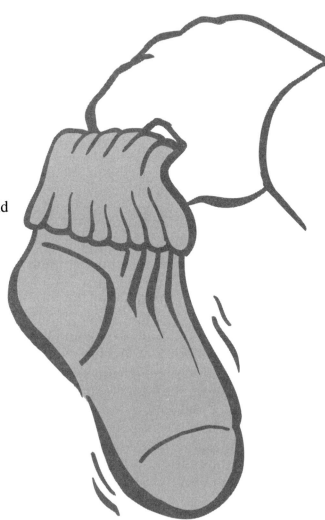

Mealtime

Pick it up.
Pop it in.
Catch the drips
On the chin.

My Drawer

Set up a drawer or a cupboard in your kitchen just for your one-year-old.

What You Need

- drawer or cupboard

- plastic measuring cups, plastic or wooden spoons, a plastic bowl, small saucepan, dish towel, any utensils that are easily manipulated and safe

What You Do

1. When you are in the kitchen, open your child's drawer.

2. Lift out one or two items and show them to your child. You might even show what could be done with the items. Say, *Look, a spoon. I stir with a spoon.* Demonstrate how you stir.

3. Put the items back and go about the business of cooking. Encourage imitation of your actions.

Soon your child will open the drawer before you do.

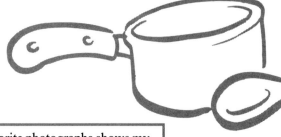

One of my favorite photographs shows my son with his pot and wooden spoon, sitting on the kitchen floor in a pile of dry spaghetti.

Exploring Tools

Your child picks up, bangs, stacks, and drops measuring cups.

What You Need

• a set of plastic measuring cups

What You Do

1. Give your child the set of measuring cups.

2. Tell about the cups.
   These are the cups I use when I cook.
   Some are big and some are small.

3. Let your child use the cups.

4. Add the cups to your child's kitchen drawer.

Try a set of plastic measuring spoons.

Pot "Music"

Bang pans and bowls for fun.

What You Need

- metal or plastic pans
- metal or plastic bowls
- a banger—wooden spoon, spatula, block

What You Do

1. Turn a pan upside down on the floor.
2. Tap the pan with a banger.
3. Set out several pans and bowls.
4. Hand your child the banger.

Try a duet.
Chant words as you tap!
*Bing Bing Bash
Hear the crash.
Bing Bing Bong
Hit the gong.*

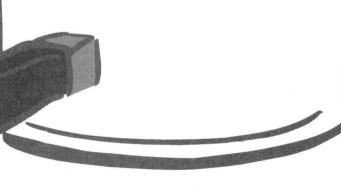

Finger Food

Picking up little snacks is good practice.

What You Need

little snacks in bite-sized pieces

- Cheerios®
- cucumber slices
- soft-cooked carrot circles
- banana, peach, or pear slices
- small pieces of soft cheese
- macaroni noodles

What You Do

1. Put your child in a high chair or on the floor.

2. Put the snack on the high chair tray or on a small plastic tray.

3. Applaud picking up and eating.

Sometimes your child may not be hungry and may see this as an opportunity for throwing. Take the clue and simply remove the snack.

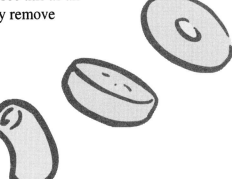

I remember one time I was making curtains for a friend. I put my one-year-old son in the high chair with his Spaghettios®. He was not hungry and decided to try out his pitching motion. The white eyelet curtains soon had a lovely orange stain in the center. It was *not* a good time for the Finger Food activity.

Pat-a-Cake Shortbread

Your child can help make shortbread cookies.

What You Need

- 8" (20 cm) baking dish
- plastic fork
- shortbread dough

Shortbread

Ingredients:
- 2 cups (250 g) of flour
- 1 cup (227 g) of butter
- ½ cup (63 g) of powdered sugar
- ¼ teaspoon (1 g) of baking powder

What You Do

1. Prepare the dough.
   Cream butter and sugar.
   Mix flour and baking powder; add to butter-sugar mixture.
   Mix well.

2. Help your child pat the dough into the pan.

3. Prick dough all over with fork. (Hold your child's hand and help with this step, if necessary.)

4. Bake shortbread 20-25 minutes at 350° (175° C).

5. Cut into squares while warm.

6. Cool and enjoy.

Recite "Patty Cake" as you cook. (see page 52)

Wash the Dishes

One-year-olds love to do what you're doing.

What You Need

- washtub with water and bubbles
- sponge or dishrag
- small plastic glasses and dishes

What You Do

1. If your child has a child-sized table or a low stool, put the tub of water on that surface. If you use a drain rack for drying, provide one for your child as well.

2. Stack small plastic dishes to be washed beside the tub and let your child take over.

3. Talk about the process.
   Rub with the sponge.
   Wash it clean.

Pudding Handprints

Enjoy this yummy printing project.

What You Need

- large plastic tray
- pudding
- plate

What You Do

1. Put your child in the high chair or at a table.

2. Put a puddle of pudding on the plate.

3. Your child presses a hand in the pudding and then presses the hand to the tray.

4. Point out the handprint on the tray. Count the fingers. Point to and name the thumb.

5. Let your child lick his or her hand.

6. Repeat until your child is tired or until the pudding is gone.

Be sure to have a camera available for a memorable shot.

Try the Texture

Eating new textures is fun.

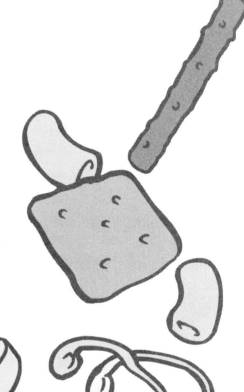

What You Need

- samples of food
- tray

What You Do

1. Put small samples of foods with different textures on a tray.
   mashed potatoes
   applesauce
   cottage cheese
   banana slices
   crackers
   pancake
   pretzels
   noodles
   yogurt
   cooked vegetables
   sprouts
   (Do not use foods that could be dangerous for your child
   such as popcorn, hot dogs, nuts, hard candy, raw vegetables…)

2. Let your child feel the foods. Talk about how the foods feel.

Remember that you can "feel" with lots of different parts of your
body—your hands, your face, your ear, and your tongue.

Indoor Playtime

Push and pull.
Roll the ball.
Line up toys
In the hall.
Stack the blocks.
Crash them too.
Watch me play
Peek-a-boo.

Play and Learn to

- develop sense of independence
- improve dexterity
- develop memory and coordination
- expand vocabulary
- learn about qualities and characteristics
- build self-awareness and confidence
- sharpen perceptual skills
- practice reaching and grasping

Activities

Notes on Safe Indoor Play with a One-Year-Old

The success of your child's play indoors depends largely upon the presence of multiple, simple playthings and the absence of hazards. Carefully evaluate toys and objects in your child's environment for any hazards.

- Light plugs should be either disconnected or covered.
- Valuable or breakable objects should be removed from reach.

- Make sure furniture is sturdy.
- Install protective guards on sharp edges.
- Store toys on a low shelf where your child can reach them without climbing.

- Put medicines and cleaning supplies in a locked cabinet.
- Keep sharp utensils, plastic bags, and garbage out of reach.

Play and Learn with Your One-Year-Old • EMC 4500

Appropriate Toys

Here are a few toys you may want to include in your child's environment. Don't push practice with any of the toys; let your child set the pace.

- blocks

- pull and push toys

- stuffed animals

- jack-in-the-box

- nonbreakable dishes

- container with cutouts and
  shaped objects to fit into cutouts

- dolls

- pounding board

- pots and pans

- pail and shovel

- small objects in a large container

- color cone with graduated rings
  (not small enough to go in the mouth)

Push a Box

One-year-olds love to push things.

What You Need

• a large cardboard box with several heavy catalogs or phone books inside
(The books will give the box stability so that it won't tip over.
Don't add so many that it can't be moved.)

What You Do

1. Put the box in an open area.

2. Put a stuffed animal in the box and push it to show how it moves. Your child may want a ride, too.

3. Leave the box where your child can choose to push it. Another day move the box to a different surface. When your child pushes it, it will have a different feel.

Talk about the pushing.

Note: Make sure child-safe gates are in place or doors are closed so that the box cannot be pushed down stairways.

Peek-a-Boo

This traditional game is always a favorite.

What You Need

• the rhyme in your head:
   Peek-a-boo
   I see you.

What You Do

1. Hide your eyes behind your hand.

2. Lift your hand, smile, and repeat the rhyme.

3. Use fans, papers, cereal boxes, diapers, or other objects in place of your hand.

4. Hide your child's eyes instead of yours.

Roll the Ball

Enjoy the fun of pushing a ball and watching it roll.

What You Need

• a soft rubber ball about the size of a soccer ball

What You Do

1. Sit on the floor across from your child. Spread your legs in a V shape.

2. Push the ball gently toward your child.

3. If your aim is good, the ball will roll into the V of your child's legs and come to a stop.

4. Your child pushes the ball to you.

5. Play as long as your child is interested. Warning: This game can go on for a long time.

Show Me

Some one-year-olds enjoy following basic directions. If yours does, try this.

What You Need

• a focused moment

What You Do

1. Sit close to your child facing him or her at the same level.

2. Say, *These are your ears,* and touch your child's ears.

3. Say, *Show me your ears.*

4. Your child responds by touching his or her ears.

5. Repeat using other body parts.
   This is your nose.
   Show me your nose.

Change the activity by saying.
   This is my nose.
   Touch my nose.

If your child gets tired of playing, stop.

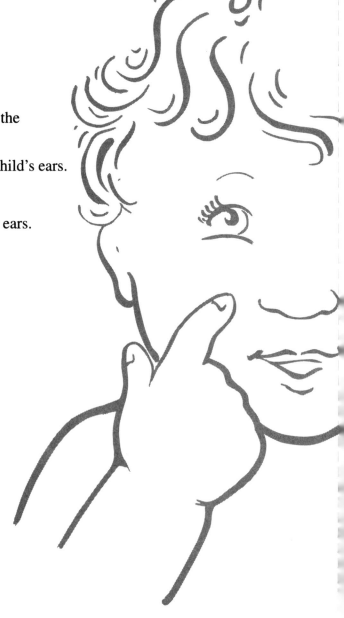

Counting Songs

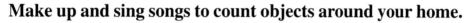

Make up and sing songs to count objects around your home.

What You Need

• a group of objects

What You Do

Sing an original version of "Ten Little Indians" to count a group of objects.

1. As you unpack the groceries,
   one little, two little jars of baby food . . .

2. As you pick up toys,
   one little, two little smiling animals. . .

3. As you fold the laundry,
   one little, two little shirts for Scotty. . .

Don't expect your one-year-old to count. Just hearing you count is an important learning experience.

Hats Off to You

Enjoy this beginning dress-up game.

What You Need

- a big mirror
- several hats

What You Do

1. Hold or sit your child in front of the mirror. Make sure that the child sees his or her image. Say,
   Look at Mark in the mirror.

2. Put a hat on your child. Say,
   See Mark's hat.
   Mark has a hat on.

3. Take the hat off. Say,
   Where's Mark's hat?

4. Repeat with other hats. Encourage your child to put on and take off hats.

If you and your child find a special "look," you may want a photograph to include in your scrapbook (page 79).

Beginning Block Play

Pick blocks up. Put blocks down. Move blocks to a new place.

What You Need

- a set of blocks

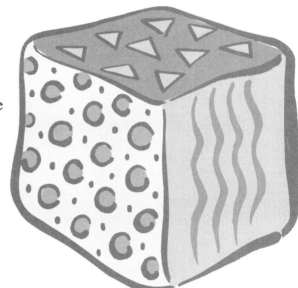

You may want to use rubber or cloth blocks that are easy to pick up. Wooden blocks should be smooth. All blocks should be big enough so that they can't be put in the mouth, but small enough to be easily picked up and put down.

What You Do

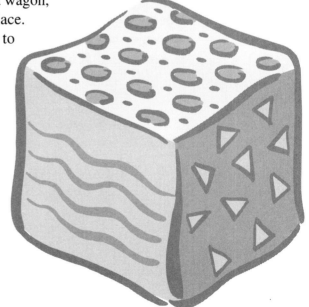

1. Provide the blocks. You may want to sit on the floor and make a row of blocks. Put several blocks in a wagon, pull the wagon, and unload the blocks in a new place. Show your child how to stack blocks. Use words to describe what you are doing.

2. Let your child explore using the blocks. Don't expect towers or walls.

Share this exploration by sitting nearby, but not by directing it.

The Line-Up

Line up stuffed toys, cars, and trucks.

What You Need

• an assortment of stuffed toys and vehicles

What You Do

1. Carry the assortment of toys to a large open area. Pick the toys up, one at a time, and put them in a row.

2. Name the toys.
    Mr. Bear, Little Dog, spinning top, truck, and *ball*

3. Put the toys back into a pile.

Don't be surprised if your toddler begins to demolish a row before it is completed. The activity is just another way to suggest picking up, carrying, ordering, and naming. You don't have to end up with an orderly row.

One-year-olds who enjoy listening to stories and looking at pictures will enjoy hearing *The Line Up Book* by Marisabina Russo; Greenwillow, 1986.

Where's My Baby?

This is a beginning version of the traditional Hide and Seek game.

What You Need

• a big item of furniture—an ottoman or a chair

What You Do

1. One day when you see that your child is behind a toy or a piece of furniture, partially hidden from your view, pretend to look for him or her.

2. Say,
   Where's my baby?

3. Look high and low, left and right, then exclaim,
   Here's my baby!

4. Lift your child and give him or her a hug.

Clay Play

Enjoy the texture of this clay as you squish it.

What You Need

• Playdough® or homemade dough

• plastic knife

What You Do

Enjoy pounding, squeezing, smashing, cutting, and tearing the dough. Don't expect your child to make anything. The process is the important part of the activity.

Watch closely to make sure that your child doesn't start eating the dough. While the dough is not toxic, it's not a good idea for one-year-olds to ingest a large amount of salt.

Homemade Salt Dough

Ingredients:
- 1 cup (125 g) of flour
- 1 cup (240 ml) of water
- ½ cup (100 g) of salt
- 2 teaspoons (8 g) of cream of tartar
- 2 tablespoons (30 ml) of oil

1. Mix all the ingredients in a pan.
2. Cook over low heat until mixture thickens.
3. Cool.
4. Knead.
5. Store in an airtight container.

Outdoor Playtime

Fill the pail and dump it out.
Push the stroller all about.
Climb and walk and splash and run.
Playing outside is lots of fun.

Play and Learn to

- practice climbing and descending
- improve perceptual skills
- learn to coordinate muscles
- look around and hear sounds
- develop sense of touch
- explore cause and effect
- sharpen conceptual thinking
- exercise perceptions of space and distance
- imitate actual experiences

Activities

Notes on Safe Outdoor Play with a One-Year-Old

Just as with indoor play, the success of your child's play outdoors depends largely upon the presence of multiple, simple playthings and the absence of any hazards. It is up to you to evaluate your child's environment for any hazards.

Outdoor play with one-year-olds should be loosely structured. Children should move freely. Parents should interact by playing beside their children, talking, pushing, swinging, and keeping the activity safe.

- Install locks on fence gates.

- Store all gardening tools and supplies in a locked shed.

- Get rid of plants and shrubs with poisonous leaves or berries.

- Set up play equipment on grass or sand, not on a hard surface.

- Cover the sandbox when not in use.

- Choose a stroller with locking wheels so that your child can climb in and out alone.

- Never leave your child unattended.

- Think about sunburns before they happen. Make sure that your child has sunblock and enough shade.

Stroller Rides

Explore new places or do your errands with your child in a stroller.

What You Need

- a stroller
- emergency bag—a diaper, wipes, water bottle, bag of snacks

What You Do

1. Load your toddler in the stroller, loop your emergency bag over the handle, and start moving.

2. It isn't necessary to move fast. Your child will simply enjoy the motion, so keep moving. Point out things as you pass them.

3. Enjoy the stroll.

When my youngest child, Scott, was one, his older brother and sister were both on a summer swim team. Scott and I put over fifty miles on the stroller as we circled swimming pools during swim meets.

Pull a Wagon

It's fun to put something in a wagon or a box and pull it from one place to another.

What You Need

- a wagon

  or

- a box with a rope handle

What You Do

1. Add a wagon (or pull-box) to your child's outdoor play area.

2. Pull your child in the wagon to show how it can be used. Talk about how it feels to ride in a wagon.

3. Give rides to several stuffed friends or other outdoor items.

Wipe and Wash

Provide a pail and a sponge so your child can do "yard work," too.

What You Need

• a small pail

• a fat sponge

What You Do

1. Next time you wash windows or clean your car, give your child a small pail of water and a fat sponge.

2. Encourage your child to sponge down a wagon, a tricycle, or even a lawn chair.

Don't expect a finished job. A one-year-old isn't concerned with the finished product.

Watering Day

The hose with water dribbling out is a wonderful toy.

What You Need

- a hose
- a rain nozzle (optional)

What You Do

1. Set up the hose in a place where water will not do any damage.

2. Let your child "water" plants, grass, bushes, shrubs, and areas of your garden.

I knew a one-year-old who wouldn't step over a hose on the ground. Johnny had to lift the hose and walk under it!

Fill and Dump

Filling a pan or a bucket with sand and then dumping it can occupy hours.

What You Need

- a small bucket or a pan

- two small plastic shovels

- a sandbox or pile of loose dirt

Make sure that your child is strong enough to dump the bucket or the pan when it is filled with sand. Choose a smaller container if necessary.

What You Do

1. Sit on the edge of the sandbox and scoop with a shovel to fill the bucket.

2. Invite your child to dig.

3. Describe what you are doing and then move to the side to let your child take the lead.

   I'm filling this bucket with sand. Then I'm going to dump the sand over there. Would you like to dig with me? I like digging.

Swinging

One-year-olds love to swing.

What You Need

• a swing

What You Do

1. Use a chair swing with a safety bar when you first swing your child.

2. Stand in front of the swing and gently pull it toward you and let go.

3. Gradually increase the force of the swing. Move to the back and push from behind.

Recite a rhyme as your child swings.

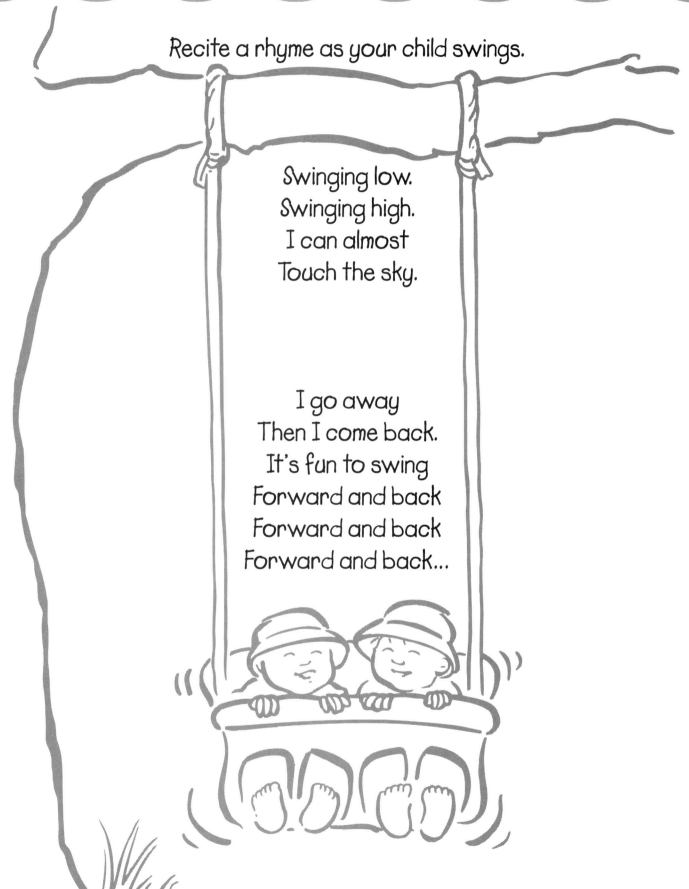

Swinging low.
Swinging high.
I can almost
Touch the sky.

I go away
Then I come back.
It's fun to swing
Forward and back
Forward and back
Forward and back...

Pounding

Provide a rubber hammer and let your child "bang" away.

What You Need

- a soft rubber or plastic hammer
- pounding board and mallet (optional)

What You Do

Note: Move things that you do not want pounded.

1. Show your child how to pound with a rubber hammer.

2. Give your child the hammer.

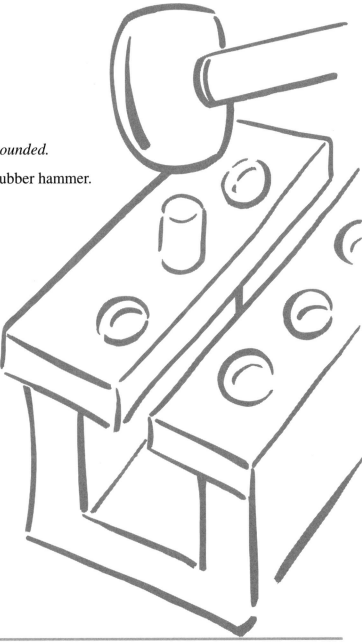

Toy manufacturers make pounding toys with pegs that can be pounded into holes. These toys are often favorites with one-year-olds.

Up, Down, On, Off

Watch your one-year-old learn about spatial relationships by exploring.

What You Need

- a place to crawl and climb

What You Do

One-year-olds enjoy moving from one spot to another, climbing, sitting, crawling, scooting up and down a ramp.

Provide a sturdy chair or piece of outdoor play equipment and the movement becomes a learning experience.

This activity can involve varying levels of difficulty.

Catch Me!

This beginning tag game is high energy entertainment!

What You Need

- an open play area (not cement or asphalt)

What You Do

1. As you and your child are playing outside say, *I can catch you.* Gently grab your child and give him or her a hug. Then put the child down.

2. Repeat several times.

3. Get down on all fours at your child's level. Ask, *Can you catch me?* Move away just a little. Your child may grab you and give you a hug.

Follow your child's lead; if he or she finds this kind of play is fun, continue. Move farther away as you ask, *Can you catch me?* Try a few simple evasive maneuvers.

Pack a Picnic

Enjoy the freedom of a picnic.

What You Need

- a container to carry your food
- food
- water, milk, or juice
- something to sit on (optional)

What You Do

Picnics are fun for parents as well as one-year-olds. Include several of your child's favorite finger foods, a large soft blanket, a bucket and a toy shovel, and plenty of liquids. Everyone is always thirsty on a picnic.

Spread out the feast and enjoy. You may take your picnic to a special destination, but going somewhere is not necessary. Your child will enjoy the picnic on your front step, in your backyard, or on your kitchen floor.

You'll find recipes for some good picnic foods my children enjoyed as one-year-olds on pages 48 and 49. Be sure to share the preparation of the foods with your child.

One-Year-Old Picnic Favorites

Finger Jell-O®

Ingredients:

> 3-ounce package (85 g) of Jell-O®
> 1 envelope of unflavored gelatin
> 1 tablespoon (14 g) of sugar
> 1 cup (240 ml) of boiling water

Dissolve the Jell-O®, gelatin, and sugar in the boiling water.

Pour into flat dish.

Refrigerate until set.

Cut into small pieces to eat.

To layer several colors–prepare one flavor Jell-O®. Put in refrigerator
to set. Prepare a second color and cool outside of refrigerator.
When the first layer is set, pour the second layer over it and return
to the refrigerator. Repeat process to create rainbow layers.

Cheese Pretzels

Ingredients:

> 1 package active dry yeast
> 1½ cups (360 ml) of warm water
> 1 teaspoon (6 g) of salt
> 1 tablepoon (14 g) of sugar

> 4 cups (500 g) of flour
> 8 ounces (90 g) of cheddar cheese, grated
> 1 beaten egg

Preheat oven to 425º (220º C).

In a large bowl, dissolve yeast with water.

Stir in salt and sugar.

Stir in flour and cheese, alternating a cup of flour with
 a handful of cheese.

Knead dough till smooth.

Form a roll.

Cut into about 30 pieces.

Roll each piece into a rope about 14 inches long.

Twist rope into pretzel shape.

Place on ungreased cookie sheet. Brush with beaten egg.

Bake immediately for 15 minutes.

To make breadsticks, don't twist the ropes of dough.

Sandwich Cubes

Make your child's favorite sandwich or try a peanut butter and honey special.

Spread one piece of bread with creamy peanut butter.
Spread a second piece of bread with honey.
Add banana slices to the peanut butter.
Put the two pieces of bread together.
Then slice the sandwich into small cubes. Enjoy.

Orange Bran Muffins

Ingredients:

⅔ cup (152 g) of butter
¾ cup (252 g) of honey
4 eggs
3 cups (375 g) of whole wheat flour
1 tablespoon (12 g) of soda
2 teaspoons (12 g) of salt
1 tablespoon (12 g) of cinnamon
1 cup (240 ml) of warm water
4 cups (244 g) of bran
2½ cups (590 ml) of buttermilk
½ cup (112 g) of raisins
1 teaspoon (4 g) of grated orange rind

Cream butter and honey.
Add one egg at a time, beating until blended.
Combine flour, soda, salt, and cinnamon. Add to
  creamed mixture alternately with warm water. Stir in bran and buttermilk.
Makes 36 to 40 muffins.

To bake, preheat oven to 375º (190º C).
Spoon muffin batter into buttered or oiled muffin pans.
Bake for about 20 minutes (30 minutes if batter has been refrigerated).

You can store batter in refrigerator for 7-10 days.
Make a fresh batch as desired.

Bedtime

Cuddle me, hug me,
Sing me a song.
Soon I'll be sleeping.
It won't be long.

Play and Learn to

- become phonemically aware
- develop memory and coordination
- improve ability to concentrate
- learn about rhythm
- explore cause and effect
- feel loved and safe

Activities

See Story Time (page 73) for additional activities appropriate for bedtime.

Action Rhymes

Chant and sing simple rhyming verses as you clap and do simple actions.

What You Need

• a rhyme in your head (see pages 52 and 53)

What You Do

When you first introduce an action rhyme, do it for your child several times. Sit your child on your lap facing you and enjoy the fun. Soon your child will imitate your actions. Applaud the attempts. Celebrate each performance.

Learn the three rhymes on the next pages. Use one or more anytime during the day when you have a quiet moment.

Play and Learn with Your One-Year-Old • EMC 4500

Three Action Rhymes for One-Year-Olds

So Big

How big is this baby?
This big? Maybe?
This big? Maybe?
This baby is so big!

Patty Cake

Patty cake, patty cake, baker's man.
Bake me a cake as fast as you can.
Roll it and prick it and mark it with B.
Put it in the oven for baby and me.

This Little Piggie

This little piggie went to market.
This little piggie stayed home.
This little piggie had roast beef.
This little piggie had none.
And this little piggie cried, "Wee! Wee! Wee!"
All the way home.

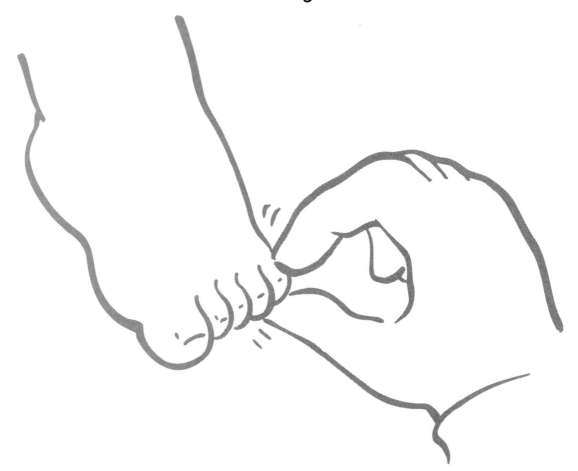

Bounce and Rhyme

Your child will enjoy bouncing to these traditional lap rhymes.

What You Need

- a lap

- strong legs

- a rhyme in your head

What You Do

1. Sit your child on your lap facing you with one leg on either side of your legs as if riding a horse.

2. Bounce your child in rhythm as you repeat the rhyme. Substitute your child's name or a relative's name in the rhyme.

3. On the final word you open your legs and let your child "fall" through. (Keep a firm hold of the child's hands as you tip him or her backwards.)

Trotty Horse

Trotty horse, trotty horse to the mill
To see Grandpappy and Uncle Bill.
Trotty horse, trotty horse to the town.
Watch out, little boy (girl), don't you fall down!

Trot, Trot to Boston

Trot, trot to Boston,
Trot, trot to Lynn,
Look out (child's name)
You're going to fall in!

This Is the Way the Farmer Rides

This is the way the farmer rides, the farmer rides, the farmer rides.
This is the way the farmer rides, so early in the morning.

This is the way the ladies ride, the ladies ride, the ladies ride.
This is the way the ladies ride, so early in the morning.

This is the way the gentlemen ride, the gentlemen ride, The gentlemen ride.
This is the way the gentlemen ride, so early in the morning.

This is the way that (child's name) rides, _____ rides, _____ rides.
This is the way that _____ rides, so early in the morning.

Bounce child a different pace for each different rider.
Bounce wildly the final time with child slipping down between your legs during the last line.

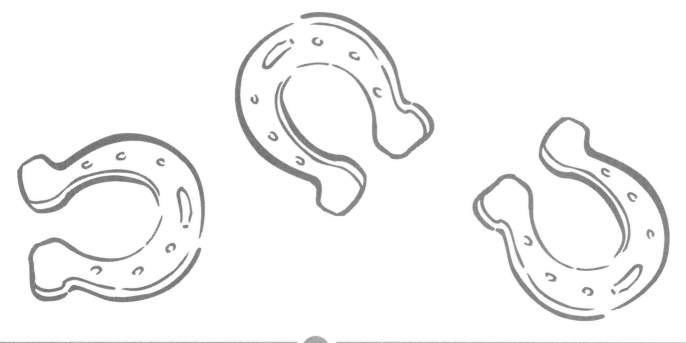

Clothes in the Basket, Blocks on the Shelf

Involve your child in picking up nightly before bed.

What You Need

• a basket for soiled clothing

• low shelving for blocks and toys

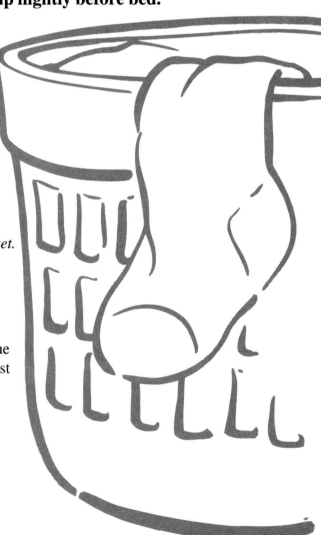

What You Do

1. Hand your child a piece of clothing and say,
   Please put this in the dirty clothes basket.

2. Describe what your child has done.
   Scotty put the shirt in the basket.

3. Be sure to thank your child for the help.

If your child is agreeable, try the same technique for placing toys on the shelves. If your child just watches, explain what you are doing. Watching is o.k.
   I'm putting the blocks on the shelf so they'll be ready for you tomorrow.

Turn Out the Light

Your child turns the lights off and on.

What You Need

• a light switch

What You Do

1. Turn off the lights and say,
   Off.

2. Turn on the lights and say,
   On.

3. Repeat.
   Then have your child move the switch.
   You say *Off* and *On*.

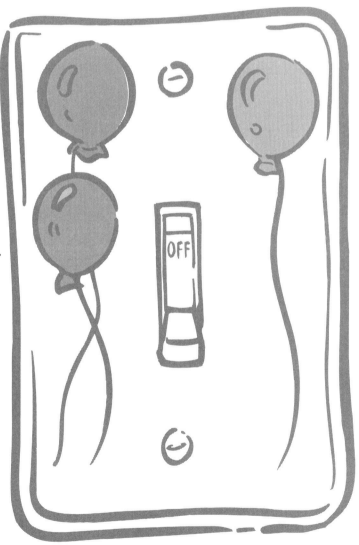

While-You-Wait Time

Waiting?
I don't mind as long as:
my tummy's full,
my pants are dry,
mommy's happy,
my bear's nearby,
there's room to roam.
If not, I cry!

Play and Learn to

- practice perceptual skills

- develop self-awareness and confidence

- sharpen memory and coordination

- develop vocabulary

- learn about qualities and characteristics

- improve dexterity

Activities

Look All Around

Enjoy the opportunity to see new surroundings.

What You Need

• the things around you

What You Do

As you wait in line or in a waiting room, point out the things around you.

1. Describe objects in simple language.
   See the big car, not *See the limousine*.

2. Make connections to things your child knows.
   There's a tree outside the window just like the tree outside our window at home.

3. If possible, walk from item to item as you talk about it.

Where Is It?

Practice memory and coordination with this simple game.

What You Need

- an object
- a blanket

What You Do

1. As your child watches, put the object under the blanket. Then ask,

   Where is (the object)?

2. Let your child retrieve the object.

3. Repeat several times, then hide the object while your child is not watching.

4. Have your child do the hiding.

Animal Sounds

Imitate the sounds that animals make.

What You Need

• pictures of animals

Use the magazines in the waiting room or the placards on the wall of the bus.

What You Do

1. Say the name of an animal or show the animal's picture. Then imitate the sound that the animal makes.

2. Ask,

   What sound does the (animal's name) make?

3. Your child answers with the sound.

Soon, you won't have to give the sound. Simply say the name of the animal and your child will give the sound.

   Play and Learn with Your One-Year-Old • EMC 4500

Take 'em Off, Put 'em On

Stuck at a meeting or an appointment without a toy? Use shoes or socks!

What You Need

• easy-to-remove shoes or socks

What You Do

This activity works better if you and your child are seated.

1. Begin by taking off one of your child's shoes.

2. Say,
   One shoe off.

3. Take the other shoe off.
   Two shoes off.

4. Put one shoe back on.
   One shoe on.

5. Put the other shoe on.
   Two shoes on.

Let your child do the taking off and putting on!

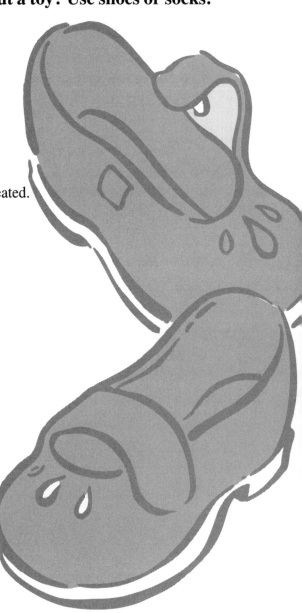

Add the traditional rhyme.
   Diddle, diddle, dumpling, my son John
   Went to bed with his stockings on.
   One shoe off and one shoe on.
   Diddle, diddle, dumpling, my son John.

While-We-Wait Toy

Add a dump-and-fill toy to your backpack to use only in waiting situations.

What You Need

- a plastic container with a lid

- 4–6 objects (big enough that they will not fit in your child's mouth but small enough to fit in the container)
  soft hair curlers
  plastic animals
  clothespins
  blocks
  measuring spoons

What You Do

1. Store the objects in the plastic container and keep it in your backpack or diaper bag.

2. When you find yourself in a waiting situation, pull out your *waiting toy*. Your child will enjoy dumping out the objects, picking them up, and putting them back in the container.

Travel Time

I think it's fun
To ride around
In my car seat
So safe and sound.

Baby Car Kit

Keep a basket or box with travel supplies in your car.

What You Need

- diapers
- wipes
- change of clothes
- sweatshirt or jacket
- blanket
- several small toys
- box of crackers

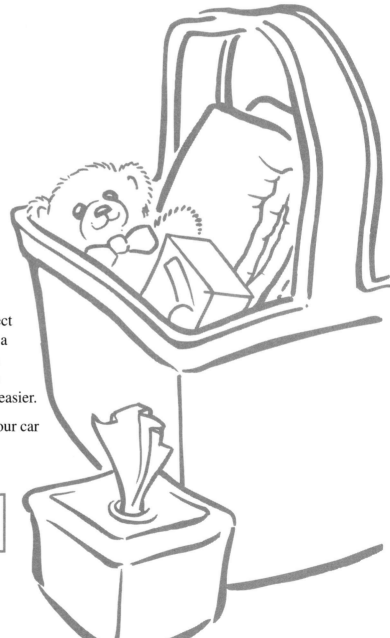

What You Do

1. Work together with your child to select and pack the items for your car kit in a basket or box. Preparing the car kit in advance will save you time and make getting ready to go somewhere much easier.

2. Help your child carry the basket to your car and find a place to store it in the car.

> *Note: Do a car kit check periodically to encourage your child to help you remember to replenish supplies in the box.*

Songs on Tape

Sing along as you listen to your favorite tape.

What You Need

- a tape
- a tape player

What You Do

1. Listen!

2. Use rear-seat speakers on long trips when the same song becomes tiresome to you.

My children's favorite holiday tape is "A Christmas Together" by John Denver and the Muppets.

Make It Fit

Your child will learn about empty and full as he or she puts socks into a container.

What You Need

- a canister with a lid (like a Pringles® container)
- several socks

What You Do

1. Give your child the canister without the lid and several socks.

2. Have your child put the socks in the canister. Show how a sock can be pushed down to make room for another sock.

3. Fill the canister, dump it out, and then count the number of socks.

4. Encourage your child to find other soft things that will fit inside the canister.

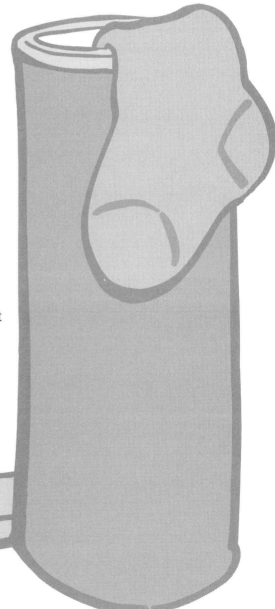

Texture Bag

One-year-olds enjoy feeling different textures—from soft and squishy to prickly and ticklish.

What You Need

- a canvas bag

- samples of materials of different textures. Choose some or all of these suggestions: satin, flannel, velvet, burlap, canvas, oilcloth, fake fur, chiffon, nylon net, and cotton batting.

What You Do

1. Put material samples in the canvas bag.

2. Give the bag to your child.
   Encourage dumping out, rubbing the different samples on a leg or cheek, looking through different samples, and hiding toys under samples and then revealing them. *(Peek-a-boo!)*

Is It in Here?

Practice putting on and taking off lids looking for a hidden treasure.

What You Need

- boxes with lids
- a small toy or stuffed animal

What You Do

1. Put the toy in a box. Replace the lids. Ask, *Where is the truck? Where could it be?*

2. Have your child find the toy. It may be necessary to hold the base of the boxes to make removing the lids easier.

3. Let your child hide the toy and you search for it.

For a special treat, wrap a new toy and put it in the box.

Rattles and Bells

Add sound to movement.

What You Need

- a bag or a box
- several rattles
- big bells

What You Do

1. Put the objects in the bag.
2. Give the bag to your child.
3. Enjoy the noises.

Try singing and
rattling together.

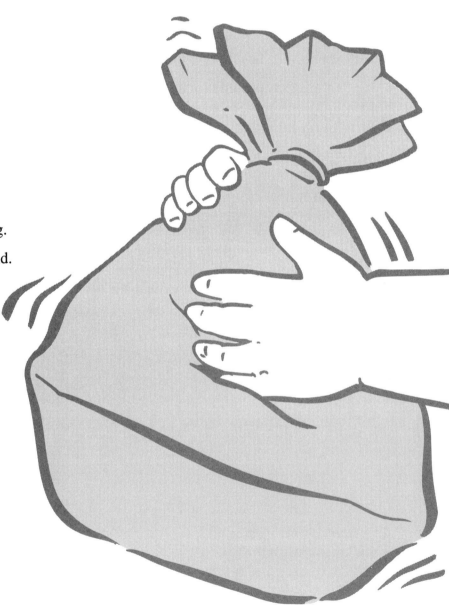

Story Time

I like the sound of
words.
I like to hear you talk.
I like it when you tell
A story as we walk.

Play and Learn to

- identify details in pictures

- hear rhythm and rhyme to
  develop phonemic awareness

- repeat words and sounds to
  extend vocabulary

- learn to identify shapes
  and colors

- sharpen conceptual thinking

Activities

Shared Reading

Sit your child on your lap or snuggle together and share a favorite book.

What You Need

- Good books!
  Try sturdy board books with clear shapes and colors.

What You Do

1. At first, choose wordless books or books with only names or labels. Turn the pages and point out the objects in the illustrations. Relate the objects to your child's experiences. Use your child's name.
   See the ball.
   Is it Tina's ball?
   Talk about your child's favorite activities.
   Look at the boy in the book.
   He has blocks just like your blocks.

2. Read from a collection of *Mother Goose* rhymes. Your child may not recognize the words, but the rhythm and the rhyme of the text will be captivating.

3. Choose books with repetition and pattern in the words and story structure.

4. Choose high-interest topics like bath and bedtime, toys, and animals.

A few suggestions:

Bookstores and libraries are filled with wonderful books for you and your child to share. There are a number of excellent read-aloud guides that will help you choose good literature appropriate to the age of your child.

Buy a few special books to enjoy over and over again at bedtime. Be sure to consider these, just a few of my favorites:

Red, Blue, Yellow Shoe by Tana Hoban; Greenwillow, 1986.

I See by Helen Oxenbury; Candlewick, 1995.

Baby Goes Shopping by Monica Wellington; Dutton, 1997.

Chicka Chicka ABC by Bill Martin, Jr. and John Archambault; Simon & Schuster, 1993.

From Head to Toe by Eric Carle; Harper Collins, 1997.

Sam's Cookie by Barbro Lindgren; William Morrow, 1982.

One of the most important things you can do to encourage a love of reading is to read to your child early.

story time • story time • story time • story time • story time • story time • story time • story time • story time • story time • story time

Tell A Teddy

Tell a story to your child's bear as your child listens and plays nearby.

What You Need

- a story
- a bear

What You Do

1. Sit down near the place your child is playing.

2. Perch your child's teddy bear on your lap and tell a story. Try a true story about your child or a traditional favorite like *The Three Little Pigs*.

Play and Learn with Your One-Year-Old • EMC 4500

Puppets

Some one-year-olds love puppets. Use a puppet to tell a story.

What You Need

- a puppet—buy ready-made ones
  or make your own (see page 78)

What You Do

1. Put a puppet on your hand. It might
   make noises or ask questions.
   Ruff-Ruff. How are you today?

2. Start talking as the puppet.

3. Move the puppet behind your back, and then
   make it reappear. Enjoy your child's giggles.

Mitt Puppet Pattern

Use an oven mitt or make a mitt from felt. Add ears and eyes and other details. Wiggle your thumb and talk with the puppet. Have the puppet sing your favorite song.

A Book about Me

Make a simple scrapbook with photos of your child's favorite things.

What You Need

- a scrapbook with several sturdy pages
- photos of your child
- photos or magazine clippings of favorite characters, places, toys, colors, and foods

What You Do

1. Put a single photo of your child on each page. It's not necessary to label or write captions, but you may if you want.

2. Share the book with your child often.

Point and Tell

Tell short stories about photographs posted on the refrigerator door.

What You Need

- photos
- magnets
- protective sleeves (optional)

What You Do

1. Put the photos in a protective sleeve. Place the copies of the photographs on the refrigerator at your child's eye level.

2. Talk with your child about the photos. Point at a photo and prompt your child to tell about who is in the picture.
   Who is that?
   What do you see in the picture?

3. Tell a true story about the photo.
   Grammy's chicken likes to eat watermelon. When Grammy goes to the chicken coop to look for eggs, she brings a piece of watermelon for the chicken to eat. It pecks the rind and eats it up fast.

Play and Learn with Your One-Year-Old • EMC 4500